I0617542

Table of Contents

Hoods of Motherhood

A Collection of Poems

Lindsay Soberano Wilson

Hoods of Motherhood

Author: Lindsay Soberano Wilson ©

Published by Prolific Pulse Press LLC

ProlificPulse.com

ISBN 979-8-9875200-6-2 Paperback

ISBN 979-8-9875200-7-9 EBook

Library of Congress Control Number: 2023904949

Published in Raleigh North Carolina USA
Paperback Publication Date: May 2023

Cover Photos: Unsplash

Author Photo Artwork by Cynthia Chapman

Acknowledgments

I Am More Than The Sum Of My Parts

Marlene In A Pub

Wings of Burden — *Age of Empathy*

In The Waiting Room — *Literary Impulse*

Monarchs Crumble — *Put It To Rest*

Little Girl Free — *iPoetry*

Mi Abuela — *Put It To Rest*

I Put It Down — *iPoetry*

I Can Rest Now — *iPoetry*

Put It To Rest — *Put It To Rest*

A Mother's Healing Touch — *iPoetry*

When I Feel Light — *Put It To Rest*

This Body Is Electric — *Literary Impulse*

Sex Miseducation — *Sensual: An Erotic Life*

Reviews

Lindsay Soberano Wilson's "Hoods of Motherhood" is a collection of deeply personal and introspective poems that offer a lyrical and evocative exploration of the themes related to the experience of motherhood, including personal history and self-care. In her poetry, Wilson contemplates the challenges of raising a child while reflecting on the impact of her family's history and trauma, including the Holocaust and the experiences of its survivors. Through her writing, Wilson engages in a healing ritual, using poetry to cleanse herself of these experiences and find solace and understanding. Her evocative language and poignant imagery invite readers to immerse themselves in the emotional landscape of motherhood, where the mundane details of daily life blend with the weight of historical memory, creating a rich and textured tapestry of human experience.

Michal Mahgerefteh, Managing Editor, Poetica Publishing

The at once soft and brash reality of motherhood is paired with the beauty and nostalgia of mothering in *Hoods of Motherhood* by Lindsay Soberano Wilson. The poet's truthful treatise on both the resilience and challenges and joy and humor of motherhood will be familiar to anyone who has been a mother or had a mother. Soberano Wilson masterfully captures the dance we mothers create as we find balance between being mothers and self-flourishing. While the poems are rooted in the experience of motherhood, fierce and tender, they catalyze the ancestral healing of past, present, and future generations. *Hoods of Motherhood* earns a permanent place on my bookshelf.

Aimee Brown Gramblin, Writer and Poet

Dedication

Dedicated to my sons, Nathan, Tyler, and Chase Wilson who are my pride and joy; and to my grandmothers, Toby Gornstein, a Holocaust survivor, and Simy Soberano, who I was named after (*Simcha* is Hebrew for joy), for both giving me eternal strength, wisdom, gratitude, nurture, inspiration, and joy.

The Eternal Child in the Mother

Now that I have this hood
I wonder when I will become
worthy enough to wear it as proudly
as a hood is worn at graduation

because there are passages:
dark passages in tunnels
there are no maps for

There are security checks:
foggy checkpoints through borders
there are no names for

There are scavenger hunts:
rigorous hunts on land
there are no rules for

This self-sacrifice is choking me
as though drowning
in this multiplying,
overflowing, mired
red-hooded gown
that keeps growing
like wild mushrooms
in *Alice in Wonderland*
or maybe
I should just *Go Ask Alice*

Hoods of Motherhood

Because I'm treading water
so as to only take the air I need
to feed or be fed upon
before the next ebb and flow
of dizzying tasks
like *Megan the Klutz*,
I stumble, fumble, and my stomach rumbles

***

Now that I have this hood
I wonder when I will become
worthy enough to wear it as proudly
as a hood is worn at graduation

Because I'm still crafting
this mask that covers the face of my past
(Some days are faceless and nameless)

I made the strips of paper-mache
out of pages from memes, tabloids,
soap operas, cereal boxes, and magazines
from *The Red Tent, The Women's Room,*
Mary Poppins, and little orphan Annie,
Little House on the Prairie, and poetry

Tell me something...
Will this always feel like a mask
or will it eventually disintegrate
to melt and meld with my face
and become me:
the eternal child in the mother.

Eau de Breastmilk and Puke

Who needs Oscar de la Renta
when I can smell like
Eau de Breastmilk and Puke

I feel like Lady Macbeth
except instead of scrubbing bloodstains
I'm frantically cleaning up
breastmilk, puke, and excrement

Only to discover it's fruitless:
because the pile of laundry grows
like *Jack and the Beanstalk*
and stalks me like a bad *deja vu*
spawning until I am lost
inside *Where's Waldo*
or maybe it's an Escher print
or better yet
a cracked Etch A Sketch.

Bath Time Ritual

As I was pouring soap onto the damp cloth
with the water running and bubbles foaming
I heard footsteps coming from the window
and I thought *"those footsteps used to be mine."*

As a girl, I used to walk by suburban homes
and hear children splashing
but it was just background music to me
as unimpressionable as elevator music.

Now, as a mom, this bath time ritual belongs to me,
so I strive to grasp this moment
but it's like water as it flows from the cup
caressing my son's body.

That crashes into someday
and someday becomes today
where I get high on nostalgia
decades after he takes showers
with the door closed.

And it all becomes background music to me again
but this time, this time
it will be as impressionable as a customized lullaby
–the lullaby I used to sing to him.

Labyrinth

some run, some walk
some crawl, some fall
some chance it, some chase it
some free swim, some do laps

(around you as you stand still
at the starting line...)

some have a map, some follow a hunch
some find the exit, some save face
some find grace, some are trapped
some watch from the outside

(as you lose yourself on the inside...)

some run, some walk
some crawl, some fall
some chance it, some chase it
some free swim, some do laps

(around you as you stand still
at the starting line...)

some have a map, some follow a hunch
some find the exit, some save face
some find grace, some are trapped
some watch from the outside

(as you lose yourself on the inside...)

The Japanese Red Maple

As spring was forcing its way
from seed
to bud
to flower
all in what felt
like the longest hour

it was also questionable
as to whether or not
what was inside
my belly
was growing or dying.

So it became
just another thing
to decipher
like the conversation
with my father
about the frail,
Japanese,
red maple
in my garden

Hoods of Motherhood

(the one he had planted
in our front yard
the one we had dug up
from my childhood home
the one on Loganberry
—yes, that special one…)

And how we were all unsure
if it would make it this year
because its buds were scarce
branches were empty
and all the while
the other flourishing trees
lined the street
to laugh at me.

"Don't worry honey.
You can just plant another one," said dad.

"I don't want another one.
I want this one," I whimpered.

I bravely turned
to the Lilac bush
and expressed my fondness
for her return
(somehow it didn't burn
as badly…).

Hoods of Motherhood

Months later,
I dug up the roots
to make room
for new life.

But I have yet
to replant
a Japanese
red maple.

I Am More Than the Sum of My Parts

The Whole is Greater than the Sum of its Parts—Aristotle

I am more than the sum of my parts
I will not hide in the dark

I am woman
mother
wife
daughter

I am mistress
slut
lover
and whore

I am who
you hate
love
and then adore

I am more than the sum of my parts
I will not hide my heart

I am woman
mother
wife
daughter

Hoods of Motherhood

I am mistress
slut
lover
and whore

I am who
you hate
love
and then adore

I am the sum of all of my parts
there is no need to hide in the dark

Wings of Burden

I'm done foraging in the woods
for bones, scraps, and maps
taking the leftovers
accepting tainted offerings
holding white flags

I'm done foraging in the woods
for hearts, hands, and sap
taking hand-me-downs
accepting unripe or spoiled gifts
holding on to recurrent dreams

Instead, I'm perched on a tree
Grounded
Faithful
Truthful
Humble
Wise
Graceful
Imperfectly Perfect

I am no longer accepting
that I need to hold
your broken wings
to fix mine
~ *those are yours to hold.*

Down With Cool Girl

Down with "cool" girl
sorry, she's not free
to be whatever it is
you want her to be.

So move on over
she wants this seat
even when you
mark it with your feet
or sit at the head
and tell her to tame it.

In fact, she just
can't contain it
and won't
bat her eyelashes
for a seat.

No, not at all—
isn't that neat?

She won't even be discreet
as she sets her own table
and won't cross her legs
or fold her arms
so you can shut down
her internal alarms.

Hoods of Motherhood

No, you can't greet her
with wet sloppy kisses
and open arms or slyly
slide up against her
as you walk on by.

No more "cool" girl
just going along
with everybody else's songs.

Down with "cool" girl
because now it's cool
to walk the walk
talk the talk
and let you gawk.

No, it's not cool
to bend to your whims
to pay for your sins.

She would rather be
a bitch
or better yet
a witch.

In the Waiting Room

This is no Bishop's waiting room
this is another kind of waiting room
one where you are unsure
which door you will use:
will it be the exit,
the delivery room,
or the D and C?

This waiting room lacks logic
and holds you hostage to dreams
that you convinced yourself
belonged to you
as the room becomes
darker, tighter, and colder
and time begins to move
in strange ways
and suddenly you're falling
f
a
l
l
i
n
g

Hoods of Motherhood

in between
waves of bellies
waves of announcements
waves of babies
waves of birthing and growing

as you sit in the waiting room
while that framed photograph you pictured
the one you first admired on your family doctor's desk
the one of the smiling parents and the three charming
children
the one where it all just seemed so complete
telling me how incomplete I am
just fades out of focus

This life must have been for somebody else
it must belong to her
like some sad story you were
meant to overhear by the water cooler.

Our Sanctuary

I used to think
the middle of the night
was reserved
for parting lovers
party-goers
and weary travelers

But now when I rouse
from slumber
shuffle into my gown
flick the night light
cuddle my baby and
burrow into the glider

I envision a collage
of women
nourishing our own

The ritual has become
habitual: his lips curled
hands unfurled
and eyes wide open
through every gulp
until his eyelids become
almond slivers

Hoods of Motherhood

And he finally exhales
or I wake halfway
through a rock
only to find he has
beaten me to it
so I guide him over
my shoulder as he is
engrossed in a stretch
rub his back and look
out the window
only to see silent blackness
sketching the sky
that has become
—our sanctuary

He then dives back
into his crib
where peace envelops
his face and as I perform
a tip-toed ritual dance
relief and accomplishment
set in

I used to think
the middle of the night
was reserved
for parting lovers
party-goers and
weary travelers

Hoods of Motherhood

But now when I rouse
from my slumber
shuffle into my gown
flick the nightlight
cuddle my baby
and burrow into the glider

I envision a collage
of women
nourishing our own

Monarchs Crumble

There's a buzz in the air
we're neither here nor there
cascading between worlds
and overlooking new horizons
into an unknown future
as monarchs crumble and stumble
like a monarch butterfly
fluttering down a new path
to the backcountry
— *the true north strong and free.*

Little Girl Free

i didn't need new dresses when i wore the weight
of others' moods and opinions
and all of the skeletons they buried deep inside of me

i'd been made to store others' guilt, shame, rejection,
pain, and hurt
for so long I allowed myself to believe I was unworthy

but that's only what they'll have you believe
because some will save themselves first
there are no *women and children first* in these parts
when they benefit from having you live in the dark

i give it back to them now —
just place all of that hate back on their laps
because it's so liberating not to wear
the weight of others' opinions and moods.

Mi Abuela

She always made me feel good enough
always made me feel
worth her love
worth her time
worth her strength
worth her wisdom
worth her touch
worth her words
worth her hope
worth her blessings

She gave me unconditional love
Unconditionally

Even if you never saw my worth
or didn't think I earned enough of her love
to cherish it the way I do

Like the warmth of the Costa del Sol
that she washed all over my aching soul.

My Bubby Toby's Secret

She doted on me
and my smooth skin
warmly touched my hands
with her worn hands
dotted in wrinkles, sunspots
lifelines and piercing veins.

There was such ambivalence
in those tender moments
when I was warmed
like savouring apple cider
and yet afraid
of the cold expiry date
that her hands told me.

(I knew by looking into her eyes
that she too
didn't know how to tell the time.)

She didn't just hold
my hands lovingly
sometimes she would
pull at them
to beg and plead
like she needed me
to hear her
in a way my mother
wasn't able to
maybe because my mom
was too up close.

But I was more removed
from the crushing weight
of being the daughter
of Holocaust survivors
of knowing they just got off
by the skin of their teeth.

Though bubby Toby
didn't like to talk about *"it"*
she still told me about it
without telling me all about it
when she repeated
her mantra to me:

"to be a somebody."

Because nobody could take
that away from me
and how getting a good education
making your own living
and being able to rely on yourself
was everything.

Sometimes she hummed it
other times she mouthed it
but mostly she breathed it
and some days
she even said it
as though our lives
both depended on it—
like it was our little secret.

I Put It Down

I put it down
I must have finally
put it down
after putting it down
so far
that it brought me down.

I put it down
I gave life to the frown
I saw the pain in the rain
the joy in the story.

There is no glory
in clutching the old story
that was never yours in the first place
So
I put it down
without a sound
drowning out underground
like a rock dropping
into the abyss.

I looked all around
at the peace that arrived
like a warm gun
when no one else was around.

Hoods of Motherhood

I think I'm still so stunned
it won't be long
Until
I rise
again…and belong.

I put it down.

I Can Rest Now

I think it's just so easy for all of you
to forget about — *all of us*
but people like me
(the mom and teacher down the street)
we carried a lot on our shoulders
we went without
we made do
to make do
for all of you

(I know no one asked us to)...

I know I gave of myself
and I guess I gave for so long
that I eventually gave up on me
so tired that I couldn't really see.

But I can rest now
I arrived at the shore
it's just that it's been so long
I forgot what it was like to walk
through my open door
to brush my hair with a new hairbrush
to buy a new wardrobe
to listen to nostalgia on repeat
to scream out loud that I made it
I can rest now
someone else has got it
I don't have to have it anymore
—I can rest now.

Put It To Rest

Put it to rest—all that you've put to the test
tear off the bandaid
that's been failing miserably
at covering up the pain

Instead, read it and name it
say it — not shame it
no matter how fragile it may be
air the dirty laundry that's been passed down
hung out to dry, strung along
and painted up in the sky

even when you crossed your heart and hoped to die
as *an eye for an eye makes the whole world blind*
Isn't that what they said?
Isn't that how we grew up?
or is that just shit they said as they stuffed it down
inside
stuffed the feelings that they tried so
desperately to hide rather than roll it all out
while kneading the dough
and ended up eating, storing, running, numbing
and rubbing feelings with thrills to flatten out the chills
like creases disappearing on finely pressed sheets

When all of this transpires
and you can see the cause of the forest fires
then you can put it to rest
bury the hatchet
as peace envelops you
like a warm, heavy, wave of humidity
the kind that would wrap you in the deserts of Sinai
washing over you like the euphoria
of surrendering your body to pleasure
and allowing it all to balance in harmony
like a key in a keyhole
suspended there in your nimble body
rocking on a hammock full of peace
— *shalom bayit.*[1]

---

[1] *shalom* means "peace" and a *bayit* is a "home" in Hebrew. Maintaining peace in one's home, *shalom bayit,* is an important ideal in Judaism.

A Mother's Healing Touch

Dedicated to the mothers of Ukraine

A mother's healing touch
is the first comfort we seek
to wash away all the pain
cradled by the *luff-luff* of the heart.

Our bodies are enmeshed
and the mind in tune
as our hearts speak to one another
with that tiny hand
gripping a mother's finger.

*(It's hard to believe
that's all we ever needed.)*

A mother's healing touch
is the comfort we seek
to wash away all the pain
when we are stunned by the bolt of a gun.

The body is shocked
and the mind is lost
the hearts struggle to speak
as the hand unfurls
seeking a warm touch.

*(It's hard to believe
that's all we ever needed.)*

Hoods of Motherhood

A mother's healing touch
is the first comfort we seek
to wash away all the pain
cradled by the *luff-luff* of the heart.

When I Feel Light

When I feel light,
I bounce like light
I fall but I don't cry
I may slip
but
like a slingshot
made of rubber, I propel
I remain untouched.

When I feel light,
I shimmer like light
I light up even the blackest of nights
I may touch the darkness
in a way that stains me
but the light beams
are an infinite source of heat.

So even when everything is bleak
there is a little light that shines on me
regardless of whether the spotlight
misses its mark or shows up
unexpectedly in the dark
like an actress on stage
who improvised her way.

Because I can always create a spark
even when playing with shadows in the dark.

This Body Is Electric

He sang her body
ʌʌʌʌʌʌʌʌʌʌʌʌʌʌ

e -l-e-c-t-r-i-c
ʌʌʌʌʌʌʌʌʌʌʌʌʌʌ

Honouring
Maternity
Nature
Divinity
and the soul

Taking only what is granted
never plundering
or mining for blood diamonds
rubies, emeralds, or gold

The female form is
ʌʌʌʌʌʌʌʌʌʌʌʌʌʌ

e -l-e-c-t-r-i-c
ʌʌʌʌʌʌʌʌʌʌʌʌʌʌ

he sang it
felt it
spoke it
to cherish
the gateway to life
in all of its wonder
curves and delight
soft and succulent
ripe and opulent
in the reflection
of ascension

Hoods of Motherhood

Your body is
ΛΛΛΛΛΛΛΛΛΛΛΛΛΛ

e -l-e-c-t-r-i-c
ΛΛΛΛΛΛΛΛΛΛΛΛΛΛΛ

wired to be admired
and hardwired to
sing siren's reveries
wrapped in longing
and moving in ways
that reveal shades of
grace
timelessness
art and
perfectionism in
imperfection

Mother and
babe as one:
babe becomes girl
girl becomes woman
all interconnected
in the seeds sown
from inside the womb

The giving force
of mother and woman
are one and the same:
you cannot honour and
feed on the one who nurtures you
as you starve the one
you take from

Hoods of Motherhood

She is waiting
somewhere in between
sound waves and heat waves
of heart waves crashing
^^^^^^^^^^^^^^^

e-l-e-c-t-r-i-f-y-i-n-g
^^^^^^^^^^^^^^^

all she tends to

She is the vessel
She is the song
~*my body is electric*

The Pilgrimage Through Your Heart

It's like you have always been you
from inception to conception
from birth to life
so much revealed
even when you were
so concealed
slowly, cautiously, and rhythmically
your personality beats
like heartbeats shooting
across a sonogram
while sipping a glass
of chardonnay on a humid
August night

At first, you were just
a newborn
stumbling out of the womb
such as a kitten —
blinded by the light
that light you now follow
religiously

Hoods of Motherhood

You, who still seems to live
inside mysteriously
and yet suddenly reveals
himself effortlessly
so that whenever you
smile, laugh, coo or cry
we say you are mine,
all mine for all of time

We knew that you would be you
but it is still too early
for you to know how to express
your excess in tune
so you sound more
like an unsynchronized
middle school band
than a refined aria
and that is why we are here
to hold your hand

But so far getting to know you
is like waking from a dream:
we can only recall some scenes
and yet somehow we
intuitively know the whole tableau
as you lie there with your arms
outstretched over your head
legs pulled up to your belly
and those slate blue eyes
gleaming into the future
as you clutch a dreamcatcher

So while you keep on walking
on this pilgrimage through your heart
just know that we are your devout
followers cheering you on
as you perfect your art.

Like a Clay Sculpture

Like a clay sculpture
your transformation
from formless to formed
from tone deaf to toned
from lifeless to alive
is wondrous to our eyes

Water, clay and loving
hands molding you
into that beautiful boy
but not everyone
you meet will help you
build and form
some will stomp, beat, and spit
and break, shame, and trip
and try to tell you who you are

Like a clay sculpture
your transformation
from formless to formed
from tonedeaf to toned
from lifeless to alive
is wondrous to our eyes

Hoods of Motherhood

Water, clay and loving
hands molding you
into that beautiful boy
but not everyone
you meet will help you
build and form
some will stomp, beat and spit
and break, shame and trip
and try to tell you who you are

But you are the artist
You are the art.

Suspended in Time

If my sense of time
has quickened with the years
and children's
sense of time
is so sincere
in its
miscalculations
and hours somehow stretch
into long summer days
then what is it like for you
baby dear

Are minutes like hours, and
sunsets like budding flowers?

If my growth has slowed
with the years
and children's growth
is measured in inches and pounds
and clothes are outgrown
and made into
hand-me-downs
then what is it like for you
baby dear

Are minutes like hours, and
sunsets like budding flowers?

Hoods of Motherhood

If my sense of touch
has dulled with the years
and children's favourite
pastime is tickle fights
as laughter emanates from
the depths of the belly
then what is it like for you
baby dear

Are minutes like hours, and
sunsets like budding flowers?

It's no surprise that time
is on your side
as you pay
it no small cost
while we make it
become our debt
slowly and willingly
the interest appreciates
and the value
depreciates
but you teach us
how to begin
again
you teach us
the value of
time.

As in the time
it may take us to do
something as mundane
as pouring our morning coffee
you are tripping over another
milestone
suspended in
time.

Isolation

Sometimes it's just me and poetry
inside these walls
How beautiful are giggles and crawls
but my mind is numb from the laps
around the mall
No matter what they say
it's just me you depend on
it's just me
it's
just
me

Sometimes it's just me and poetry
inside these walls
How beautiful are giggles and crawls
but my mind is numb from
Thomas the Train on repeat
No matter what they say
it's just me you depend on
it's just me
it's
just
me

Sometimes it's just me and poetry
inside these walls
How beautiful are giggles and crawls
but my mind is numb
from holding my breasts on a platter

Hoods of Motherhood

No matter what they say
it's just me you depend on
it's just me
it's
just
me

Roll Over, Roll Over

At first, I did it for you
guided you with my hands
trying to make you
understand just where you
could land

We had been practicing
for just over a week
when I used Sophie
the Giraffe to coax you

I sang, "There were ten in the bed
and the little one said, roll over, roll over..."
when you bent your left elbow
and used your right arm as an oar
wiggled your legs like flippers
until you landed
flat on your back—splat!

With a blase look on your face
while I doted on
your small feat and feet.

A Case of the Napping Blues

I've got a case of the napping blues
O the napping blues
Just when you thought
it couldn't get any worse:
baby staged a walk-out
Up-down, shush-pat, break my back
that little baby can be a brat!

When you have the napping blues
it's fight or flight
fight him to the end
or take flight and let him win

When you have the napping blues
nothing falls into place:
the dog barks on the walk
the garbage truck talks
the construction men ram their drills
and the doorbell shrills

I've got a case of the napping blues
O the napping blues
Just when you thought
it couldn't get any worse:
baby staged a walk-out
Up-down, shush-pat, break my back
that little baby can be a brat!

Night Waking

Here I am again:
night waking
I am his for the
taking
I thought we said
goodbye
This night is no friend
of mine

They call it a
developmental
milestone
I call it mental
1 month, 2 month
3 month, 4
I thought you were done
asking for more
I thought maybe, just maybe
we had closed
that door

This night is no friend
of mine
I thought we said
goodbye
I am his for the taking:
night waking.

Our Walking Ritual

I know when the cars are tucked
into their driveways
and when they are on a commute

I know where the construction zones are
to avoid drills, bangs, saws, and grinding

I know how the sun hits the stroller
and at what hour and for how long

I know when to emulate the night
by draping a blanket over the top of the sun shield

I know where you like to be strolled
on the newly paved asphalt in figure eights

I know how you also like going over
the rhythmic bumps of the sidewalk cracks

But now the seasons are changing
leaves are descending, the sunshine is ending
and our walking ritual will have to hibernate

That is until the mud pokes through the snow again.

Peace

When my second-born son
wasn't here
his absence was loud:
the nursery room loomed
the crib mocked
the glider balked

When he finally
arrived, he was silently
placed in my arms:
there was no big bang
he just floated into our lives...
a growing family...

My eldest son's 5th birthday
was marked without the weight
of the losses hovering over us
like the broken spine of the almanac

Today, my second-born son
is just like that:
he fills the room
with quiet medicine power
as I sheltered him
from the numbness
I had enveloped myself in
just to survive

Hoods of Motherhood

Because the pain
doesn't go away:
it's a sound machine
on replay
but the calmness
the gentleness
that comes from my son
keeps it at bay
still

We now rock back and forth
to the music
back and forth
on the glider
back and forth
on the waves of my life

I can feel him now
I can hear him now
That peace he brought
to my wrestling heart
His Hebrew name:
Samuel, means *God has listened*

But others wrestle
that demon for a lifetime:
Bring peace to the noise
love to the heartache
and compassion
to the story you know not of.

Hold On to That Sweet Note

Entering more disarray
has invited me to rise
as though this was how
I was meant to mother:
in between the intricacies
of baby, toddler, and boy
dividing myself
across my loves
so that somehow
there isn't division
only multiplication
of all that I have to give...

...If I can just hold on
to that sweet note
when I feel overrun...

I take solace in the
laughs and horseplay
cascading
through my home
in the ripped blue jeans
messy T-shirts
and hockey sticks
because boys are my lifeline
running through the door
asking of me
asking for me...
asking me for more...

Hoods of Motherhood

*...If I can just hold on
to that sweet note
when I feel overrun...*

I Birthed in 20 Minutes, She Tweeted

After all
of the refining
and redefining of
Motherhood
some of us still brag
and wear
our birthing stories
like a badge
of honour
an honour roll
and role
rolling words into spit
balls of raging fire:
Natural
and arrived in
20 minutes flat,
she tweeted…

…F
a
l
l
i
n
g…

…at the soles
of feet
and the souls
of wombs
who are
Unnatural,
I presume

Because
my first baby boy
arrived after
24 hours
before I accepted fate
made it a date
could hardly wait
even when
Cesarean
won the war

My second baby boy
arrived after
7 hours
before I accepted my fate
I went on the date
could hardly wait
even when my
battle scars were
unstitched and
restitched

My third baby boy arrived
after 1.5 hours since
this time there was no
tempting fate
instead, I made a pact
by scheduling a date
as I had enough
on my plate

Do I win
something now?

Goddess

When the sculptor
becomes the sculpture
the artist
becomes the art
the lover
becomes the love
and the god
becomes the goddess
out of the ashes
of the Virgin
that was Mary
and the *fatale*
that was *femme*
comes a spirit
who was held
captive
like Rapunzel wrapped
in vines
and hurled
with stones
by her, him, them and they
and what they say ~
always getting in the way

The goddess has lived
as a shapeshifter
of evanescence
and iridescence
for far too long
bending and singing to
everyone else's song:
good girl, bad girl and
even *Little Girl Lost*
until she uses the stones

Hoods of Motherhood

she collected to
turn them into dust
becoming a sculpture
donned in nudity
and floral wreaths
grounded in the beauty
beneath her dainty
feet
bathed in consent
respect, and power
is the goddess
waiting to be served

She will walk with you
if you honour her
she will hold you too
if you let her
she will stay with you
if you build her a home
~ so honour the goddess
within.

Sex Miseducation

They will have you teetering on
the tightrope of fear
before they tell you
anything real
before they prepare you
for a miscarriage
before they prepare you
for a negative pregnancy test
before they prepare you
for a stillbirth
before they
prepare you.

Before they prepare
you they will have you teetering
on the tightrope of fear
before they tell you
how or that you
can enjoy yourself.

No, that's not spoken about.
No, pleasure does not exist:
don't speak of it
don't name it
don't think of it
don't dream it
don't be it
and certainly don't do "it."

Hoods of Motherhood

So they will have you teetering on
the tightrope of fear
before they tell you what it's like,
or where to get an abortion,
or how to know if you want one.

No, that's not for you
that's for them and that's a sin.
We don't talk about that or this
or this or that
and that's a fact.
That's a matter of fact.

We don't like that.
You don't want to be that. That.
That's that.
That's a matter of fact.
Fact.

Keep Theology Out of Our Biology

Keep theology out
of our biology
these body politics
have me thinking
of all the riots
that flew by us
somehow we surpassed
that then came back
like a snag
on a pashmina
but it's my uterus
snagged by father patriarchy
suffocating
mother matriarchy
redefining autonomy
telling us what
should and shouldn't be

a part of me
and how it's not my body
to own

Hoods of Motherhood

That somehow
whether viable or
nonviable
we are primed to be
handmaids
sowing the threads
of our submission
held hostage by
the Commander
commanding policies
found in newsprint
running and smudging
fading and staining
like rationed coffee beans
somewhere in my great aunt's
basement

Keep theology out
of our biology.

Alive to Thrive

Breaking and fixing
digging and building
cracking and repairing
falling and landing
tripping and leaping
cutting and taping
melting and shaping
drafting and polishing
prepping and cooking
dying and birthing
dreaming and living
planting and flowering
surviving and thriving ~
alive to thrive.

Voice Box

I tore, ripped, crumpled, and then
flattened out every page
that was ever written about me
or I ever ghostwrote about myself
and stacked them all up
way up
and then lined them all up
all up
and finally guided them down
way down
into the sharp claws and jaws of the shredder
marveling at the voice box
submerged in piles of paper strips
I managed to compile
of unreleased compilations.

Permission

she gave
herself
permission

to be

her best

—her—

not better than...

Stolen Moments

how many stolen moments
make up a day

a sip of coffee
a glance at the paper
a jotted note
a poem
a jaunt
a phone call

we steal these moments
as though we need to
steal
moments that belong
to us
sealed with an oath
returned to sender.

Delirium

Night runs into day
and day runs into night
especially when you have
no more fight
but sometimes it's not just
in the day to day affairs
but month runs into month
and year runs into year
and unless you stop running
from the blurry daze and haze
that envelopes these days in a maze
then they would be none the wiser.

But you will be —you will be wiser.

I Am a Pandemic Zombie Mom

No, I won't just join
your online group
for beauty products
for women who are living

I am a pandemic zombie mom
sometimes I feel as though
I don't belong

A sip of lukewarm coffee
is my nail salon
A warm bath that the kids
jump into is my spa
A pizza night delivery
is my restaurant

You get the picture, don't you?

Lockdown after lockdown
school shut down after school
shut down
it's any wonder I get any
shut-eye
I try and try and try but then
I cry and cry and cry
because it's been too long
just getting by

Hoods of Motherhood

Snack after snack, grocery
run after grocery run, laundry
after laundry, clean up
after clean up, play outside
after we play outside
play inside after we play
inside after playing inside
always inside on the outside
of our own lives

You get the picture, don't you?

I am a pandemic zombie mom
I try to stay strong
to help the kids with all that's going on
and all that goes wrong
when they scream and yell
about how this is all hell
(if they're not telling me to go to hell)
when they say they hate
these stupid masks
when they cry at night
and don't know why
when they name people and places
they miss that I didn't even know exist
when the screen makes them mad
it makes me so sad
to know I birthed zombie babies

I am a pandemic zombie mom
sometimes I feel as though
I don't belong.

Metamorphosis

Sitting in the hollow of time
not really feeling like that life was mine
had to tread through the swamps
mop up the slosh
look green monsters in the eye
because they twisted my neck so high
to stalk me in my own home
like that bear in the dream
letting itself in
threatening my offspring
tainting the beauty inside
until I pulled out the long entangled snake
running through my body
down my throat
burrowing and burying rooms
inside organs, I didn't even know I had
until the poison erupted
and I threw it all away
took down the family photos
rummaged through the trash
among the packing boxes
and cut my wrist on glass ~ a slit ~
but eventually, I felt the stitches dissolve
and shed the bandage
to wear the new skin
~ love the skin you're in.

J'adore

Something tells me
that the way I love you
consistently
unconditionally
absolutely adoringly
and devotedly
will make you want
to share long after
you graduate from
baths to showers with
the doors closed
and then locked

That you will want
to share long after
you graduate from
diplomas and degrees
with honours
and then accolades

That you will want
to share long after
you marry from
engagements to the
honeymoon phase
and then first homes

Hoods of Motherhood

That you will want
to share long after
you make your own
house a home
with children and families
and the neighbourhood friends

Something tells me
that if I cared then you
will want to
one day share
all that you
adore and more

I would like to think
because I loved you
harder that you will
want to stick
around more.
~ *J'adore.*

Ice Queen

Even though she had to drown
without even ever making a sound

in a frozen Muskoka Lake
wearing an unruly mane

of blue crystallized icicles
from the top of her head down to her toes

where the underworld's deep freeze
lived inside of her as heavy as black ice.

~

Even then, she still found a way
to float back up with the muddy spring thaw

like that overflowing styrofoam cup
as boundless as the sea

with her untamed mane of washed-out locks
lost in the loch ness monster of her heart

after scouring the bottom of the pack
for promises broken and unborn.

~

That is when she met resolve to dissolve
into the fog of murky green algae waters

Hoods of Motherhood

like a puzzle, she tried to solve from afar
that looked clearer as winter drew further

and she drifted like an iceberg to spring's embrace
to take her home despite the fear in her pace

like Juliet contemplating her fate in a vial
hanging from a sterling silver chain.

~

It was on that day when she saw the reflection
of a melting Ice Queen that her fate was sealed

and she walked through the industrial-sized freezer
nursing her cold heart to health and wealth

as she floated back to life with the hummingbirds
of spring healing from the fight, flight, and freeze

to live again in green buds and phosphorescence
blooms on lush wreaths and vines that thrive alive.

Utopia I Have Seen

Utopia I have seen
in a glimmer, in a dream
in a moment of pure bliss
from a lover's kiss
or
a baby's suckle

Utopia I have seen
in a glimmer, in a dream
in a moment in between
the setting sun
or
fresh honeydew

Utopia I have seen
in a glimmer, in a dream
in a moment where I am free
inside a marriage vow
or
witnessing baby's first steps

Utopia I have seen
in a glimmer, in a dream
in that moment I'm serene
beneath her dress
and
hoisted upon his chest

Now My Voice Box Echoes

And here I was thinking
rediscovering my voice box
at the bottom of a paper shredder
full of pages of shit other people
said to me or about me
was enough

But that was only step one
because I've since found
that the voice box echoes
what you tell it
what you yell at it
what you whisper to it
what you will it

I've since then found
that the voice is growing
as it echoes
around me
inside of me
surrounding me
protecting me
from those who tinker with it

Now my voice box echoes
back to me
and it sounds like me
instead of tricking me
into letting others
speak for me.

Divine Motherhood

Dedicated to my loving mother

She didn't only carry me in the womb:
she carried me through the years and the fears
from diapers to walking shoes
from cabbage patch dolls to initial rings
from training bras to graduation caps
from not knowing myself

to thinking I knew myself
to getting to know me
to getting to know a new self
to relearning all I knew about myself

She was the anchor
between the waves of discord
when all I could do was destroy life
as a teenager —unhinged
but her hood didn't wear
she kept the lifeline beating through

the wrong boyfriends
the wrong jobs
the wrong makeup
the wrong friends

Hoods of Motherhood

Then when I arrived at my own
womanhood
I dragged her across Europe
backpacks in tow
marched the streets of Venice, Nice, Florence
Rome, Cannes, and Pesaro
finding strength in treading newfound terrain

When my wanderlust wouldn't fade
she followed my heart to Israel
digging for passion, love, and life
reclaiming roots we hadn't planted yet —
finding them entangled in dank soil
mired in hopeful tears
sowed by her mother
and her mother's mother
and her mother's mother:

a shrine of yellow stars, pogroms,
perogies, borscht soup, gold jewels,
sheer stockings, lace gloves, gramophones,
hair dye, and Shabbat candles
tightly wound in a satchel of silent martyrdom

Hoods of Motherhood

I thought I knew her
I thought I knew her well
That was until I arrived at my own motherhood
and all of the self-sacrifice, love, worry
despair, joy, hope, pain, pride
all wrapped up together:
past, present, and future
held so heavily deep, deep inside
striving to remain poised
struggling to reclaim jewels and discard shadows
of collective trauma that mires our hoods

From not knowing myself
to thinking I knew myself
to getting to know me
to getting to know a new self
to relearning all I knew about myself

Motherhood so divine
giving so much that one day you find
you need to take the time
to untangle what's really yours
from what's really mine.

The Wise Mother

Mother in the hood
don't despair
even though
you don't think
you don
or own
the wear
it's your hood
what you make of it
what you take of it
what you give to it.

This picture right here:
this is me
I call this motherhood…
tired eyes so dry and hazy
heart so full yet so shaky
from all the adrenaline
I convert into energy
to nurture those
under my hood
of protection
nowhere near
Perfection.

Hoods of Motherhood

Mother in the hood
don't despair
it's all yours to wear
sometimes it fits snug
beyond compare
other times it gives you a tug
or a hug
or falls to your feet:
old and tattered
and incomplete.

Until you sew it back together again
and then again and yet again
leaving your fingers bleeding,
punctured, and bruised
yet able to play again and again
and yet again—
I call this motherhood.

I called this motherhood
until
I learned
how to also be a mother
to myself
just like mother nature
instead of plundering
from myself
I gave
back to myself

Hoods of Motherhood

and only then
did I learn
how to mother
and heal
my inner child
to peace.

About the Author

Lindsay Soberano Wilson is the proud mother of three boys. She is a poet, and a high school English teacher. She is also the editor and creator of *Put It To Rest*, a mental health literary magazine, where writers put their personal stories to rest. Her chapbook, *Casa de mi Corazón: A Travel Journal of Poetry and Memoir*, explores how her sense of community, Canadian Jewish identity, and home was shaped by travel. Her poems have appeared in *Fine Lines Literary Journal*, *FreshVoices*, *Embrace of Dawn*, *Poetry 365*, *PoetryPause*, *Quills Erotic Canadian Poetry Magazine*, *Canadian Woman Studies Journal*, *Fevers of the Mind*, and *Poetica Magazine*. She holds a MA (English) and a BEd from the University of Toronto, and a BA (Creative Writing and English) from Concordia University.

Follow her at:

poetrymatters.medium.com

lindsay.soberano.wilson on Instagram

matters_poetry on Twitter

Lindsaysoberano.com